TOMMY RO
BIOGRAPHY

The Controversial Life and Legacy of Britain's Most Polarizing Activist — Free Speech, National Identity, and the Battle Over Modern Britain

Mark A. Robinson

Copyright @ 2025 by Mark A. Robinson

All rights reserved. No part of this publication may be reproduced, distributed or transmitted in any form or by any means, including photocopying, recording or other electronic or mechanical methods, without the prior written permission of the publisher, except in the case of brief quotations embodied in critical reviews and certain other noncommercial uses permitted by copyright law.

Disclaimer

This book is a work of biography and journalism. It is based on publicly available records, interviews, court documents, media reports, and credible sources. While every effort has been made to ensure accuracy and fairness, some events, conversations, and personal experiences have been interpreted to provide narrative coherence and context.

The author does not endorse any political beliefs, actions, or opinions expressed by Tommy Robinson, his supporters, or his critics. The inclusion of quotes, incidents, or perspectives is intended solely for informational and analytical purposes, to present a complete picture of the subject's life and the societal context in which he operated.

Readers are reminded that legal, social, and political opinions about Tommy Robinson vary widely. This book does not serve as a guide to legal matters, activism, or political action. Any legal interpretations, descriptions of court proceedings, or representations of events are based on available public information and may not reflect all perspectives or outcomes.

All names, organizations, and events described are used in good faith for the purpose of factual biography and historical record. The book respects privacy where possible but prioritizes public interest and historical accuracy in chronicling the life and influence of its subject.

Table of Contents

Prologue

Luton Beginnings

The Making of an Outsider

Searching for a Cause

Founding the EDL

Street Protests and Media Storms

Inside the EDL

Exit from the EDL

From Activist to Public Enemy

Behind Bars

The Digital Battlefield

The Journalist Incident

The Political Arena

The Global Stage

Family, Faith, and Identity

Supporters and Opponents

A Mirror of Britain

Epilogue

Prologue

A Nation on Edge — The Arrest That Shocked Britain

The morning air was unsettled, charged with the kind of tension that precedes both celebration and violence. Outside Leeds Crown Court, the crowd swelled along the narrow pavement, spilling into the road despite the barriers erected to contain them. Flags fluttered in the breeze—some stitched with the red cross of St. George, others hand-painted with slogans scrawled in block capitals. The chanting rose and fell in waves, sometimes jubilant, sometimes threatening, as though the crowd itself could not decide whether it was gathered for a parade or a reckoning.

Police had been stationed early, their vans positioned like chess pieces across the surrounding streets. Uniformed officers leaned on shields, scanning the faces before them with a wary detachment born of experience. They had been here before—at marches, at protests, at rallies where anger simmered into confrontation—and they understood that one word too sharp, one move too forceful, could set off a chain reaction no one could control.

Inside the courthouse, a different kind of tension unfolded. Journalists tapped notes into phones and shuffled papers, sensing that something beyond a routine contempt of court hearing was unfolding. Few charges inspire much public passion, yet the defendant was no ordinary man. Tommy Robinson—born Stephen Yaxley-Lennon—was already a figure who divided Britain with unusual ferocity. To some, he was a truth-teller who exposed the hypocrisies of government and media. To others, he was a provocateur whose rhetoric courted hatred and inflamed division. His name alone was enough to spark arguments across pubs, classrooms, and family dining tables.

When Robinson emerged from the building, cameras lifted in unison. He was trim, square-jawed, dressed in a fitted suit that hinted at the calculated performance he understood so well. He glanced at the waiting crowd, his eyes narrowed as if measuring their energy, drawing strength from the cheers of loyalty that cut through the noise. Reporters surged forward, microphones extended, questions hurled in rapid fire, though none could be answered before the officers closed in.

The arrest was swift, almost mechanical. Two policemen approached from behind, their hands locking around his arms in practised motion. The crowd erupted—shouts of betrayal, chants of resistance, curses directed at the police. Robinson struggled only briefly, more for show than escape, his voice rising above the commotion as he proclaimed the injustice of the moment. In that instant, he knew the cameras were capturing him precisely as he wanted: a defiant figure being dragged away by the State, a man punished for speaking.

The police van's door slammed shut with a metallic thud, and the image that circulated across the world was sealed in that moment: Robinson's face pressed against the glass, his lips moving in words that could not be heard but needed no translation. It was the picture of a man turned symbol, a man whose supporters would claim him as a prisoner of conscience and whose critics would cite as a menace finally facing consequence.

Within hours, the scene had moved far beyond Leeds. Social media erupted in fury, with hashtags demanding his release gaining global prominence. Demonstrations broke out not only in London but in Berlin, in Melbourne, and even in Washington, where his name was invoked in speeches about liberty and censorship. Petitions gathered signatures at a pace usually reserved for humanitarian crises. For his detractors, this was confirmation that he had mastered the art of manipulation, turning even his punishment into propaganda. For his admirers, it was evidence of a truth so dangerous that only silencing could contain it.

But the meaning of the moment could not be understood by the arrest alone. It was the culmination of years in which Robinson had become a vessel for Britain's anxieties: fears of terrorism after the London bombings, anger over grooming gangs that had gone unpunished, resentment over immigration in towns that felt transformed overnight. He had placed himself at the centre of all these storms, sometimes with calculation, sometimes with recklessness, always with the instinct that controversy was both his shield and his weapon.

The Leeds arrest was not his first, nor would it be his last, but it became the one that crystallised the debate over who he was. Was he a working-class patriot silenced by an out-of-touch elite? Or was he a dangerous demagogue exploiting grievances for personal notoriety? The question itself revealed the fracture running through the Country, a fracture that seemed to widen each Time his name appeared in the headlines.

The van carrying Robinson disappeared into the distance that morning, but the arguments it ignited continued long after. Families split over him. Politicians avoided his name in Parliament even as they debated the issues he raised. Newspapers devoted endless columns to analysing his following, his strategy, and his future. His presence, whether behind bars or behind a camera lens, had become inescapable.

This biography does not begin with that arrest simply because it was sensational. It starts there because it was symbolic. It captured the essence of the man and the moment: an arrest that became an emblem of a nation's unease, a single scene that distilled years of cultural conflict into a few charged minutes. From the housing estates of Luton to the global stage, from street marches to social media networks, Robinson's journey is inseparable from the story of modern Britain's turmoil.

To understand how the country reached the point where a single man's courtroom violation could spark protests around the world, one must return to the world that shaped him, long before he was a symbol, when he was simply Stephen, a boy growing up in a town already beginning to change.

CHAPTER 1

Luton Beginnings

The story of Stephen Yaxley-Lennon, who would later adopt the name Tommy Robinson, begins not with the roar of a crowd or the flashing of cameras, but in the quiet disarray of a town that seemed perpetually in decline. Luton, the Bedfordshire town where he was born in November 1982, was once a proud industrial hub. Chimneys and factory roofs had dominated its skyline, the kind of place where a man could leave school on a Friday and start work on a Monday with little more than grit and a pair of boots. By the time Stephen was a child, however, that world had collapsed. Car plants closed, manufacturing jobs evaporated, and the town's confidence withered with them.

What remained was a population searching for purpose. Communities that had been stable for generations were now fractured, as waves of immigration brought new languages, foods, and religions to streets that had once seemed familiar. For some, the change was welcome—a sign that Britain was modern and open. For others, especially those who felt left behind by economic decline, it felt like displacement, as though the town itself had slipped from their grasp. Luton became a kind of microcosm of Britain's late-twentieth-century struggles: the collision of working-class tradition with globalisation and multiculturalism.

Stephen was born into this churn. His family background was Irish Catholic, his grandparents having come to England during the mid-twentieth-century waves of migration that brought thousands from Ireland to the factories of Luton. Like many such families, they carried with them the dual burden of being both insiders and outsiders—workers needed for their labour, yet frequently treated as second-class citizens in the communities where they settled. That paradox would seep into the boy's earliest understandings of identity. He grew up British but also aware of being marked by heritage, part of the perpetual negotiation of belonging that defined working-class immigrant life.

His father was largely absent from his early years, and his stepfather, a man who worked in the motor industry before its collapse, became the figure of authority in the household. His mother provided stability where she could, though her son's restless energy often tested her patience. Home life was modest, shaped by the rhythms of council estates where families lived cheek by jowl, gossip moved quickly, and respect was hard-won.

From a young age, Stephen revealed himself to be both intelligent and combustible. He absorbed the world around him with a sharpness that surprised his teachers, but he also bristled at authority. In the playground, he was quick to defend himself, sometimes with words, sometimes with fists. Fights were not unusual in Luton's schools, where children from different backgrounds—white working-class, Pakistani, Bangladeshi, Afro-Caribbean—jostled for space and respect. For a boy growing up in the 1980s and 1990s, the divisions of the adult world often replayed themselves in miniature on the football pitch and in the corridors of comprehensive schools.

Stephen's Irish heritage also carried echoes that he could not fully articulate as a child but would later recognise. The Irish community in Britain had long lived with suspicion, particularly during the years of the Troubles when bombings in London and Birmingham hardened attitudes. Though the Irish of Luton had worked hard to establish themselves, they still carried the weight of being a minority viewed through the prism of violence and unrest. For Stephen, this meant growing up with the sense of being an outsider even within the majority population. That feeling of marginality—of belonging and not belonging at once—would later form the bedrock of his worldview.

The school provided its own tests. He attended Putteridge High, where he was neither the star pupil nor the delinquent, but something more complicated: bright enough to see through the drudgery of lessons, restless enough to rebel against their structure. Teachers often remarked on his quick tongue, his refusal to back down, and his ability to rally other children to his side. He was, in short, a natural leader, though not always in ways that authority figures welcomed.

Trouble was never far away. By his teenage years, Robinson had already begun to brush against the edges of law enforcement. These were not the kind of major crimes that made headlines, but the petty scrapes familiar to many working-class boys: scuffles outside pubs, minor altercations with rival groups of youths, the occasional run-in with the police that ended with a warning rather than a conviction. Yet each encounter deepened his resentment of authority. To him, the police seemed less like guardians of order and more like intruders into the natural hierarchy of the street, where respect was earned through defiance rather than compliance.

Still, his early years were not defined entirely by conflict. Football provided an outlet, as it did for countless boys of his generation. On Saturdays, he followed Luton Town, the local club whose fortunes had dimmed but whose matches remained a point of pride for the town. The terraces taught lessons of loyalty, toughness, and belonging that school could not. It was there, in the chants and camaraderie of fellow fans, that he first experienced the intoxicating power of collective identity. This lesson would stay with him long after he left the stadium.

By the time he approached adulthood, Stephen had grown into a young man marked by contradiction. He was sharp enough to hold down an apprenticeship as a bricklayer, eager enough to work, yet restless enough to find himself in constant skirmishes. He was proud of his heritage yet uneasy about how identity was shifting in his town. He was ambitious but without a clear path forward, tethered to a community that seemed to be drifting without direction.

The boy who would become Tommy Robinson had not yet found his cause. But in the restless streets of Luton, surrounded by the scars of industrial decline and the tensions of multicultural change, the conditions for his transformation were already in place. The town's struggles mirrored his own—fractured, angry, searching for stability in a world that no longer resembled the one promised to generations before.

It was from this soil that the activist would grow, not yet as a leader of movements or a household name, but as a restless young man shaped by an environment that seemed always on the edge of confrontation.

CHAPTER 2

The Making of an Outsider

As adolescence gave way to adulthood, Stephen Yaxley-Lennon stepped into a world that seemed both familiar and precarious. For a boy from Luton in the late 1990s, the traditional path forward was through skilled labour, the trades that had sustained working-class families for generations. Stephen took up an apprenticeship as a bricklayer, and in the rhythm of mortar and stone, he found a craft that offered both pride and a means of survival. His hands hardened quickly, the skin roughened by lime and dust, his muscles strengthened by the repetition of lifting, measuring, building. Bricklaying demanded discipline and focus, and for a Time it provided him with the stability that school never had.

On building sites across Bedfordshire, he learned more than technique. He absorbed the culture of the trades: the camaraderie of men sharing flasks of tea on scaffolds, the unfiltered language that served as both humour and hierarchy, the pride in work done well even when the wider world seemed indifferent. It was a culture rooted in loyalty, toughness, and self-reliance, the kind of values Stephen carried instinctively. He was good at the work, quick to learn, proud to show he could keep pace with men older and more seasoned. In those years, bricklaying was not just a trade but an identity, a mark of being part of the backbone of Britain's working class.

Yet the stability of work did not erase the turbulence beyond the jobsite. Luton was a town divided, and nowhere was that division sharper than among its youth. The decline of industry had left boredom and unemployment in its wake, and from that void gangs emerged, groups of young men bound by geography, ethnicity, or shared grievance. Street corners became contested ground, football rivalries bled into personal feuds, and the town seemed perpetually on the brink of confrontation.

Stephen was drawn into this environment almost naturally. He had the temperament for it: sharp-tongued, quick to react, unwilling to back down when challenged. His Irish heritage had already given him the instinct to fight for respect, and the estates of Luton demanded nothing less. Local gangs formed along lines that mirrored the town's demographic shifts—white working-class youths on one side, groups of South Asian descent on the other. Tensions often flared not from ideology but from the simple fact of proximity: young men competing for space, status, and safety in neighbourhoods where mistrust ran deep.

Stephen found himself in the middle of these clashes more than once. Fists, bottles, and insults were standard weapons, and though most of these fights were short-lived, they left their mark. He was no stranger to the blue lights of police cars or the bark of officers breaking up a brawl. For him, these encounters were not merely physical contests but early lessons in belonging and division. The sense grew that his community was embattled, that forces contested the ground under his feet that he did not control.

It was during this Time that the seeds of resentment began to take root. In his eyes, the authorities seemed either indifferent or biased. When grooming scandals later broke across the Country, revealing years of abuse ignored by officials, Robinson would point back to these years in Luton as proof that the system had failed. Long before such revelations made headlines, he carried the impression that police and politicians looked the other way, unwilling to confront uncomfortable truths for fear of offending minority communities. To the young man working his trade by day and clashing with rivals by night, this was not abstract politics but lived reality.

The apprenticeship gave him a sense of craft and pride, but it did not insulate him from these growing convictions. The work was honest, but the evenings and weekends told a different story: a town where identity was increasingly at the heart of conflict. Stephen began to frame his experiences not only in terms of personal battles but in terms of cultural struggle. The divisions of the street became, in his mind, the divisions of a nation. He was part of one side, and the other was encroaching.

Football deepened this perception. Supporting Luton Town was more than sport; it was an arena where identity was asserted with chants, flags, and sometimes fists. Rivalries were colored not just by team loyalties but by the demographic divides that marked the town. To be a Luton lad was to stand shoulder to shoulder with those like you, against whoever stood opposite. On terraces and in alleyways after matches, Stephen saw the power of collective identity, how individuals could dissolve into a single voice, a single force.

These experiences hardened him. Though still in his teens and early twenties, he was already beginning to see himself not simply as a tradesman or a youth among many, but as someone marked by conflict, an outsider who understood truths that others ignored. He had not yet articulated this in speeches or slogans. Still, the outlines were visible: a belief that the working-class white community of towns like Luton was under pressure, overlooked, and dismissed.

By the Time he completed his apprenticeship, Robinson had acquired more than a skill. He had absorbed the lessons of a community in tension, lessons that fused pride in honest work with anger at perceived injustice. The building sites taught him discipline; the streets taught him defiance. Together, they shaped the man who would soon step into activism, not as a politician trained in debate halls, but as a fighter forged in the everyday struggles of a town that mirrored the Country's own fractures.

The outsider was taking form, not yet as a leader of movements, but as a young man convinced that he had seen something others refused to see. In Luton's shifting streets, the seeds of identity politics had been sown, and Stephen Yaxley-Lennon carried them with him, ready to be cultivated when the Time came.

CHAPTER 3

Searching for a Cause

The restless energy of Luton in the late 1990s and early 2000s offered few places of belonging for a young man like Stephen Yaxley-Lennon, the boy who would one day be known to the public as Tommy Robinson. By the time he entered his late teens, the routines of apprenticeship and working life as a bricklayer were already proving too narrow for the fire that burned inside him. His town, with its tightly packed neighbourhoods and streets heavy with tension, provided its own forms of distraction and, often, confrontation. In that combustible atmosphere, Robinson began to search for something larger than himself, some outlet through which his discontent could take form.

One of the first arenas where he found both camaraderie and conflict was football. Luton Town FC, the club that embodied local pride, was more than a team. Its stadium, Kenilworth Road, was a crucible of working-class identity. To stand on the terraces and roar for the Hatters was to declare allegiance not only to a club but to a community that saw itself as embattled and overlooked. Yet football culture at the Time carried a darker undercurrent. For a teenager already drawn to defiance, the chants, the rivalries, and the ritual of standing shoulder to shoulder with other young men became intoxicating. Robinson was swept into the subculture of football hooliganism, a world where fists, pride, and belonging collided.

The stadium clashes and street skirmishes were more than simple brawls. They were expressions of a larger malaise. Britain was shifting, towns like Luton were changing, and many young men felt that their place in society was slipping away. For Robinson, these skirmishes were an initiation, teaching him about loyalty, strength, and the power of numbers. They also hinted at the possibility that anger, if organised, could be transformed into something larger than a scrap outside a pub.

Parallel to these experiences, Luton itself was becoming a stage for deeper cultural and religious debates. The town's sizable Muslim population, many of whom had roots in Pakistan and Bangladesh, brought with them traditions, businesses, and institutions that reshaped entire neighbourhoods. Most families sought stability, education, and a future for their children; yet, the visibility of cultural differences grew more pronounced against the backdrop of wars abroad and headlines about radical clerics preaching in Britain, tensions at home sharpened.

Robinson's personal grievances, rooted in clashes he claimed to witness between different groups in Luton, began to merge with this broader narrative. His anger was no longer simply about being looked down upon as a working-class lad or finding release in a Saturday fight. It was taking on a political hue. He began to see himself as part of a larger struggle, though at first he lacked the vocabulary or structure to define it.

Moments of confrontation in his neighbourhood became formative. Arguments outside takeaways, scuffles after nights out, and whispered stories of radical preachers at local mosques began to shape a worldview that saw his town not as a place of integration but of fracture. In his telling, there was a growing imbalance, one that he feared left traditional communities vulnerable and voiceless. Whether these impressions were entirely accurate or exaggerated by the charged atmosphere around him mattered less than the fact that they hardened his sense of mission.

It was during this period that Robinson first became drawn to activism. He attended small demonstrations, sometimes local in scale, other times connected to broader campaigns against extremism. These early steps were tentative, a far cry from the headline-grabbing protests he would one day lead, but they marked the beginning of a transformation. He was learning that politics, however messy, could channel the same adrenaline as the terraces, but with a reach far greater than a Saturday fight.

The personal was now becoming political. The grievances of a young man who felt his community was under siege merged with the anger of a generation that believed leaders in Westminster had abandoned it. Robinson, restless and eager for a cause, was beginning to discover the power of organised protest. It would not be long before he placed himself at its centre.

CHAPTER 4

Founding the EDL

The moment that set Tommy Robinson apart from thousands of other disillusioned young men in Britain did not arrive with fanfare. It came quietly, almost impulsively, in the summer of 2009, when simmering frustrations found an outlet and coalesced into a movement that would soon draw headlines around the world. By then, Robinson had already lived through the discontent of Luton's streets, the violence of its football terraces, and the sting of being told that the concerns of people like him carried little weight in a political culture that preferred silence to confrontation. What had been private anger and local grumbling was about to become public defiance.

The catalyst was an incident that might have seemed small at first glance: a protest by a group of Islamist radicals in Luton against British soldiers returning from service in Afghanistan. To Robinson, the spectacle was not just offensive; it felt like a desecration of loyalty to Country, a calculated insult aimed at the very people risking their lives for Britain. The images of banners calling soldiers "butchers" and "baby killers" circulated quickly, igniting fury in households already sceptical of immigration and suspicious of multicultural policies. For Robinson, it crystallised everything he believed was wrong with Britain's political class: that extremists could flaunt their hatred while ordinary citizens were expected to watch silently.

The rage that day was raw, but unlike many of his peers who shouted from the sidelines, Robinson sought to harness it. Out of informal conversations in pubs, text messages exchanged among friends, and late-night rants that blurred into strategy sessions, a loose circle began to form. They were not polished politicians or ideologues with manifestos. They were bricklayers, mechanics, security guards, and young men with bruised knuckles from football matches. What bound them together was not theory but a sense of betrayal—of being sidelined in their own towns, of feeling that their pride in Britain was branded as bigotry.

The name came quickly: the English Defence League. It was blunt, unambiguous, and resonant with working-class men who felt they had been defending themselves for years without recognition. The term "defence" was crucial. It implied that they were not aggressors but guardians, protectors of a culture they believed was under siege. The choice of "league" evoked camaraderie and structure, something that could elevate their anger into collective action.

Initially, there was little organisation. Meetings were held in pubs or car parks, where strategy was discussed over pints. The earliest marches were crude affairs, patched together through word of mouth and crude online postings, with men turning up draped in flags and chanting slogans. Yet within weeks, Robinson discovered something remarkable: the numbers kept growing. Every time a demonstration was held, more men appeared, eager for a chance to give voice to their frustrations. Some came from Luton, others travelled from towns that bore similar scars of deindustrialisation and demographic change.

The mainstream press dismissed them as thugs and racists, a label that only hardened their identity. To Robinson, the hostility of journalists and politicians was proof that they had struck a nerve. Each condemnation served as confirmation that the establishment did not want their grievances heard. And while outsiders saw only chaos in the chants and confrontations, Robinson sensed an opportunity to give direction to what might otherwise have been aimless fury.

The appeal of the English Defence League lay in its simplicity. It did not require members to read political tracts or align with traditional parties. It required only the conviction that something precious was slipping away from Britain and that standing by was no longer an option. In council estates and factory floors, the message spread that finally, there was a movement prepared to say out loud what many muttered in private.

The spark of 2009 ignited a fire that would not easily be extinguished. Robinson's instinct had been correct: discontent was everywhere, waiting for a banner under which to march. What began as improvised anger in the streets of Luton was transforming into a national spectacle. The EDL was born, not in a conference room with policy papers, but in the heat of outrage, the camaraderie of the terraces, and the determination of one man who believed that silence was no longer possible.

CHAPTER 5

Street Protests and Media Storms

The year after the English Defence League first took to the streets, Britain found itself staring at a new political theatre, one that erupted not in Parliament or in television studios, but on high streets, in city squares, and outside mosques. Demonstrations became the EDL's calling card. Crowds of men, many in football shirts, marched behind banners declaring opposition to Islamic extremism. The chants were loud, often crude, and always designed to provoke. Yet behind the aggression lay something more complex: a sense that working-class voices had been silenced for too long. Tommy Robinson, by then the undisputed figurehead, stood at the centre of it all.

The EDL's first significant protest in Birmingham in 2009 offered a template for what would follow. Violence broke out after rival groups clashed, leaving images of smoke, police lines, and bloodied faces splashed across front pages. For supporters, the chaos was proof that they had touched a nerve in a nation refusing to confront uncomfortable truths. For critics, it confirmed their worst fears: that this was the rebirth of a far-right street army in modern Britain. Robinson rejected the label, arguing that his movement targeted Islamic extremism, not ordinary Muslims. Yet the optics told a different story, one that the press seized upon relentlessly.

Each demonstration became part-political rally, part-pantomime, and part-riot. Crowds gathered in Newcastle, Manchester, Bradford, and London. Counter-protesters from Unite Against Fascism and other anti-racist groups turned out in equal force, ensuring almost every EDL event ended in confrontation. The cycle became predictable: the EDL announced a protest, opposition groups mobilised, police erected barriers, and by day's end, arrests were made.

The television cameras rolled, ensuring millions who had never seen Robinson in person now recognised his face.

Robinson quickly learned how to play to those cameras. He gave interviews in which he styled himself as an ordinary man forced into extraordinary circumstances, someone defending his community because politicians had abandoned it. His speeches, often delivered from the top of makeshift stages or police vans, blended anger with a curious charisma. He was not polished; his delivery was raw, filled with blunt metaphors and the cadence of the football terraces. But for his followers, this was the point: he was one of them, speaking their language, airing grievances that academics and politicians dismissed as crude or unspeakable.

The media, however, framed him differently. National newspapers called him a thug, a demagogue, and a dangerous populist. Broadcasters placed him alongside Europe's rising far-right leaders. Robinson bristled at such portrayals, insisting he opposed racism and repeatedly pointing out the group's Jewish, Sikh, and even Muslim members. Yet the tension between message and method was hard to escape—videos circulated of EDL supporters chanting inflammatory slogans, drinking heavily, and clashing with police. Even when Robinson condemned the violence, his association with the spectacle defined him.

For the police, the EDL was both a logistical nightmare and a public order crisis. Every protest drained resources, costing millions of pounds in security. Robinson was summoned repeatedly to court, facing injunctions, fines, and bail conditions that restricted his travel. Yet each arrest only deepened his legend among supporters. They saw him as a man harassed by the State for daring to speak the truth.

At the same time, Robinson's visibility grew internationally. His speeches and interviews circulated online, drawing the attention of like-minded activists in Europe and the United States. The label "far-right" stuck, yet his insistence on being an anti-extremist campaigner complicated the narrative. The ambiguity became part of his appeal. To some, he was a courageous truth-teller. To others, he was the embodiment of dangerous nationalism.

The years of street protests turned Robinson into a household name, but they also boxed him into a corner. The very tactics that won him attention also alienated much of the public. As the clashes multiplied, it became clear that the EDL could never transition into a mainstream political force. Robinson himself would later acknowledge this, recognising that the media spectacle, while powerful, left his movement branded in a way that no amount of rebranding could erase.

For Britain, the EDL years forced a reckoning. Television viewers could not avoid the images of working-class men chanting outside mosques or the headlines warning of rising extremism. Robinson had made himself impossible to ignore. Whether loved or loathed, he had carved a place in the national conversation.

By the end of this period, Tommy Robinson was more than just a local activist from Luton. He had become a symbol, his name synonymous with both resistance and rage. The protests gave him a platform, but they also set in motion the battles—with the media, the law, and the State—that would define the next stage of his life.

CHAPTER 6

Inside the EDL

The English Defence League grew quickly, much more rapidly than even its founder could have anticipated. What had begun as a furious reaction to a single demonstration in Luton spread into a patchwork of divisions across Britain. Within months of its founding, groups in Birmingham, Manchester, Newcastle, and beyond were staging their own rallies under the same banner. For those who felt they had been pushed to the margins of British society, the EDL offered a sense of belonging. For others, it provided an outlet for anger that had simmered without direction for years. But inside the movement, cracks began to show almost as soon as it had formed.

At the heart of the EDL was a culture of defiance. Meetings and rallies were less about careful planning and more about solidarity in opposition. Many of its members were young men with working-class backgrounds, people who had grown up in towns transformed by immigration, struggling industries, and declining wages. The pub, the football terrace, and the street were their familiar arenas, and the EDL gave them a stage to bring all those worlds together. It was not uncommon for a demonstration to resemble a football away day, complete with chants, flags, and a volatile edge that often spilled into violence. This blending of football culture with political protest made the EDL distinct, but it also seeded a destructive element that Robinson himself found increasingly complex to control.

Leadership weighed heavily on him. Robinson had never set out to be a politician, and he lacked the infrastructure of a formal organisation. Decisions were often made on the fly, guided more by instinct than by strategy. He positioned himself as a reluctant figurehead, a voice for ordinary people rather than a polished leader, yet he was the one to whom cameras and journalists turned. That visibility came at a cost. Every misstep by an EDL member, every moment of chaos at a rally, was projected onto him personally. In the public imagination, he was the EDL.

Inside the ranks, divisions festered. While Robinson envisioned the EDL as a movement against Islamist extremism rather than Islam itself, many who joined did not share that distinction. There were factions openly sympathetic to far-right ideology, individuals who saw in the EDL a platform to push racist or fascist views that Robinson claimed to reject. This clash of intentions left the movement fractured, with some chapters drifting toward extremism and others trying to maintain the message of opposition to radical Islam alone. Robinson spent much of his Time putting out fires within his own organisation, expelling members who went too far, issuing statements to distance himself from those who tarnished the group's image, and trying, often in vain, to assert control.

The friction was not confined to the membership. Robinson's encounters with the police became a defining feature of the EDL's existence. Each protest drew a massive police presence, draining public resources and escalating confrontations between demonstrators and officers. To the authorities, Robinson was a troublemaker who incited unrest. To his supporters, he was a man hounded by a State unwilling to listen. The clashes hardened his conviction that Britain's institutions were biased against people like him, a belief he repeated in interviews and speeches with increasing intensity.

The press proved another adversary. Newspapers and television reports rarely distinguished between Robinson's stated aims and the behaviour of his most aggressive followers. To journalists, the EDL was a far-right street movement, no different from previous incarnations of extremist politics in Britain. Robinson railed against this portrayal, insisting that he was trying to highlight failures in immigration policy and the dangers of Islamist extremism, not to stir up racial hatred. Yet the images splashed across front pages—burning flags, drunken crowds, police in riot gear—told another story, and it was that version which stuck in the public mind.

Government pressure soon followed. Local councils worked to ban demonstrations, and courts imposed restrictions on Robinson himself. Travel bans, injunctions, and arrests became routine, feeding his reputation as both a lawbreaker and a martyr. Each restriction became, in his telling, further proof that the establishment feared him and the movement he represented.

Inside the EDL, Robinson's authority was both absolute and fragile. Supporters looked to him as the face of resistance, yet many resented his attempts to moderate the group's message or distance it from outright racism. The more he tried to control the movement, the more it slipped beyond his grasp. By 2011, he was locked in a battle not just with police, press, and politicians, but with the very people who had once rallied to his side.

The English Defence League had given Robinson a platform and notoriety, but it also became his burden. He was trapped in a cycle of confrontation that he could neither fully embrace nor easily escape. What had started as a protest movement against one incident in Luton had grown into a national force that carried his name and his image, for better or worse. Inside the EDL, he found both power and isolation—a movement too large to abandon, yet too fractured to lead truly.

CHAPTER 7

Exit from the EDL

By 2013, Tommy Robinson's relationship with the English Defence League had grown increasingly fraught. The movement he had founded out of anger and ambition had become something he could no longer fully control. What began as a local protest against extremist demonstrations had ballooned into a national phenomenon, complete with its own hierarchies, factions, and internal politics. Robinson's leadership, once charismatic and reactive, now felt like a constant negotiation, a series of compromises and confrontations that weighed heavily on him.

The reasons for his departure were both practical and personal. Within the EDL, splintering factions had emerged, each with its own interpretation of what the movement stood for. While Robinson had consistently framed the organisation as opposition to Islamist extremism rather than Islam itself, some chapters veered into overtly racist and far-right rhetoric. For him, the public association with violent, extremist factions undermined the very message he hoped to communicate. Every headline of brawls and arrests reinforced the perception that the EDL was a street gang, not a protest movement with a political conscience.

Pressure from authorities compounded the internal strife. Robinson faced repeated arrests, injunctions, and bans that restricted his travel and public speaking. Demonstrations, once the lifeblood of the EDL, became logistical nightmares, costing millions in policing and drawing relentless media scrutiny. To his supporters, these were signs of persecution; to Robinson himself, they highlighted the unsustainable nature of the role he had taken on. The energy required to manage both a fracturing movement and a hostile legal and media environment was exhausting.

Amid this turmoil, an unexpected opportunity emerged: the Quilliam Foundation, a counter-extremism think tank, reached out with the possibility of partnership. Their mission, focused on combating radicalisation through education and advocacy, offered Robinson a chance to step away from the street-level chaos while reframing his public image. He engaged with the foundation, participating in interviews and public discussions aimed at exploring pathways away from extremism. It was a chance, he believed, to reinvent himself as a constructive voice in the debate over Islamism and British identity.

Yet the experiment proved difficult. Robinson struggled with the constraints of working within an institutional framework. The Quilliam Foundation emphasised measured language, careful framing, and research-driven policy—qualities at odds with the instinctive, confrontational style that had defined him for years. His audience, accustomed to his unfiltered rhetoric, often rejected the moderated voice. Social media, which had once amplified his street protests, now became a venue for criticism from former supporters who accused him of selling out. The transition was awkward and, ultimately, unsustainable.

Despite leaving the EDL formally, Robinson's notoriety did not fade. The media continued to treat him as a polarising figure. Each appearance, whether in interviews, online videos, or courtrooms, reminded the public of his previous role as the face of Britain's most prominent street movement against Islamist extremism. The departure from the EDL had freed him from internal factional disputes, but it had not freed him from public scrutiny. Indeed, leaving the organisation seemed to solidify his reputation; he was no longer just a protest leader, but a symbol, a touchstone in national debates over free speech, security, and identity politics.

Robinson's exit was therefore a paradox. He had created a movement that thrived on anger, chaos, and defiance, yet those very qualities made continued leadership untenable. Quitting the EDL offered a chance at reinvention, a path toward legitimacy and reflection.

Still, it could not erase the years spent in the public eye, nor the associations forged through confrontation and spectacle. In leaving, he traded control for freedom, yet the world refused to let him slip quietly into obscurity.

By 2013, Tommy Robinson had stepped away from the movement that had made him famous. But stepping away did not mean stepping down. His life had been transformed by the visibility, the controversy, and the relentless energy of the EDL years, and the story was far from over. Leaving was only the beginning of a new phase—one defined less by street protests and more by media attention, legal battles, and the ongoing negotiation between public persona and private ambition.

CHAPTER 8

From Activist to Public Enemy

After stepping away from the English Defence League, Tommy Robinson's life entered a new and more perilous chapter. The streets were no longer his primary battleground, but the attention he had amassed over years of protests, confrontations, and media coverage ensured that he could not fade into obscurity. Instead, he became a figure defined less by what he built than by how the State, the press, and the public responded to him.

The media quickly cast him in stark terms: not as a concerned citizen or former activist, but as a provocateur, a man whose words and actions threatened public order. Headlines labelled him "far-right," "controversial," and, at times, "dangerous." Television debates often painted him as emblematic of a rising tide of extremism in Britain, regardless of the nuance he attempted to present. Robinson learned quickly that public perception could be as powerful as any street protest. A single misstep, a brief speech, or a confrontation captured on video could define him for millions who would never meet him in person.

Legal entanglements became a constant in his life. Arrests, injunctions, and court cases piled up, often for actions that, to his supporters, were symbolic acts of defiance rather than criminality. Whether for contempt of court, public order offences, or accusations of incitement, Robinson found himself repeatedly before the judiciary. Each trial, each headline, and each prison sentence amplified his notoriety. The State, intentionally or not, was turning him into a public figure of extraordinary visibility, someone who occupied the intersection of law, politics, and media spectacle.

The cycle of arrest and release created a narrative in which Robinson's supporters and detractors saw entirely different realities. To those who followed him online or attended his events, he was a martyr, harassed for daring to speak what they considered inconvenient truths. To critics, he was a dangerous provocateur whose presence on the national stage encouraged division, fear, and occasionally violence. This dichotomy amplified every action. Every court appearance became more than a legal matter; it was a media event, a chance for Robinson to reinforce his narrative while opponents framed it as proof of wrongdoing.

Political establishments also felt the pressure of his notoriety. Politicians from multiple parties were forced to respond, often in defensive terms, while think tanks, academics, and journalists dissected his rhetoric and his influence. Robinson's persona became a test case for debates over free speech, extremism, and community cohesion. The very visibility that had once made him a street-level agitator now placed him at the centre of national conversations. Each protest he had led, each video he had uploaded, each speech he had given in the prior decade became part of a growing dossier that defined him in the public imagination.

Meanwhile, the division among the public deepened. Working-class communities, especially in towns like Luton, viewed Robinson's actions through the lens of shared experience. To them, he was speaking truths that politicians and the media refused to acknowledge. To middle-class observers and the broader political establishment, he embodied intolerance and extremism, an unsettling figure who leveraged grievance into a platform of influence. Britain, already navigating the strains of economic instability, multicultural integration, and globalised media, now found itself polarised by one man's public presence.

The very tools of modern communication accelerated Robinson's transformation from activist to public enemy. Social media amplified his voice far beyond the street protests where he had cut his teeth. Videos of speeches, confrontations, and arrests circulated internationally. Supporters rallied online, creating a digital echo chamber that magnified his influence and protected him from complete marginalisation. At the same Time, journalists dissected every statement, legal teams monitored every action, and opponents mobilised campaigns to neutralise his impact.

In this stage of his life, Robinson became a symbol more than a man. The struggles that had begun in the streets of Luton, through football terraces and council estates, had escalated into national and international prominence. Every arrest and legal challenge reinforced the polarities of public perception. He was simultaneously a hero to some and a threat to others, a figure whose notoriety could not be ignored and whose influence had outgrown the movement he once led.

By the mid-2010s, Tommy Robinson's identity as a public enemy was fully cemented. The street activism of the EDL years had evolved into a complex web of media attention, legal scrutiny, and political debate. He had become a man whose life, every decision, and every word were under constant observation. What had started as a restless young man seeking a cause in Luton had transformed into a national flashpoint, forcing Britain to confront questions of identity, freedom, and the limits of dissent.

CHAPTER 9

Behind Bars

By the mid-2010s, Tommy Robinson's battles had shifted from the streets to the courtrooms, and eventually to the stark confines of prison. Legal troubles that had long shadowed him came to a head, culminating in multiple arrests and convictions that drew intense media attention. To supporters, the courts were yet another arm of a system intent on silencing a truth-teller. To detractors, they were a necessary measure against a man whose rhetoric and actions had repeatedly crossed legal boundaries. In both cases, the result was the same: Robinson's life became inseparable from the spectacle of justice itself.

The prison sentences were varied. Some stemmed from contempt of court, particularly when reporting on sensitive trials, while others were tied to public order offences accrued over years of demonstrations. In every instance, Robinson insisted that the charges were politically motivated, portraying himself as a victim of an establishment eager to suppress dissent. These claims were carefully amplified through social media, interviews, and supporters' networks, turning each court appearance into a public event far larger than its legal significance.

The official narrative, as framed by courts and law enforcement, painted a different picture. Judges and prosecutors cited repeated violations of court orders, public disorder, and actions that risked undermining the legal process. Police statements emphasised the challenges of maintaining public safety during demonstrations where Robinson had been involved. Yet the more the authorities detailed their case, the more Robinson and his followers portrayed it as censorship. Every prison sentence, every court ruling, was reframed in online forums and videos as proof that the British State would stop at nothing to silence him.

Prison itself was an environment of intensity and isolation. Robinson faced not only the physical constraints of incarceration but the psychological weight of constant scrutiny. Media crews, supporters, and detractors alike dissected every moment. Letters and social media posts became lifelines, tools to maintain his narrative and reassure followers that he remained defiant. Yet the experience also exposed him to the harsher realities of confinement. Surveillance, regimented schedules, and the company of men from every corner of Britain—including those whose own crimes were violent or petty—tested his resolve daily.

The period behind bars paradoxically strengthened Robinson's public profile. Supporters rallied in response to each sentence, organising protests outside prisons and online campaigns that highlighted alleged mistreatment. His incarceration became a symbol of resistance, a rallying point that reinforced the dichotomy of hero and villain in the public imagination. Every story of solitary confinement, restricted access, or denied privileges was transformed into evidence of persecution, regardless of the official record.

Meanwhile, Robinson's critics remained unsparing. Legal experts and journalists scrutinised every claim, comparing allegations of mistreatment with prison logs and court documents. The debate over truth versus perception intensified. For the public, the question became less about whether Robinson had broken the law and more about whether the State's response was proportionate. In this crucible of media scrutiny and legal contention, the narrative of imprisonment became a defining chapter in his life.

Even as prison walls confined him physically, they could not contain his influence. Videos posted online, statements released through lawyers, and interviews given upon release allowed Robinson to maintain an almost constant presence in the public eye. The spectacle of incarceration amplified his platform rather than diminishing it. For many of his supporters, prison was a badge of honour; for his critics, it underscored the consequences of his activism.

In this stage of his life, Robinson became a figure both larger and more polarising than ever. Behind bars, he was at once isolated and omnipresent, his every move analysed and debated, his story transformed into a symbol of defiance. Prison did not silence him; it reframed him, casting his struggles within a narrative of persecution and resilience that would continue to fuel his notoriety for years to come.

CHAPTER 10

The Digital Battlefield

As traditional avenues of activism became increasingly constrained, Tommy Robinson discovered a new frontier: the digital world. Where once the streets of Luton or the crowded terraces of football grounds had provided him with visibility, now platforms like Facebook, YouTube, and Twitter offered reach that was instantaneous and global. Here, Robinson was no longer bound by police injunctions, permits, or local authorities. The internet became both his amplifier and his arena, allowing him to speak directly to an audience that could not be contained by geography or law.

Robinson's digital strategy was deceptively simple. Videos of speeches, interviews, and rallies were uploaded with precision, often timed to coincide with breaking news or court developments. Posts were designed to provoke, inform, and energise. Each upload carried a dual purpose: to maintain the loyalty of existing supporters and to attract new followers who might feel unheard or overlooked by the mainstream media. Through social media, Robinson could bypass traditional journalists entirely, controlling the framing of his own narrative and creating a loyal digital base that rivalled the crowds he once drew to the streets.

But the digital landscape also expanded his audience internationally. European right-wing activists, American alt-right figures, and libertarian commentators took note. Robinson became a figure in a transnational network of like-minded individuals, exchanging interviews, appearances, and online support. In countries like Germany, Sweden, and France, activists mirrored his strategies, while in the United States, his rise was closely watched by figures associated with online conservative media. Social media did not just amplify his voice domestically; it elevated him to a global stage, where the issues of extremism, immigration, and free speech were contested in parallel debates across continents.

The digital battlefield was not without risk. Platforms became increasingly hostile to content that violated rules on hate speech, harassment, or incitement. Robinson's accounts were repeatedly suspended, banned, or restricted. Each ban triggered an outcry among supporters, reinforcing the narrative of censorship and persecution. To many of his followers, the removal of his posts or channels was evidence that the establishment feared his message, validating his claims of being silenced for speaking truths others avoided.

Robinson's social media empire, however, was never invulnerable. Algorithms shifted, content moderation became stricter, and platforms faced pressure from governments and advocacy groups to curtail incendiary material. As one network after another imposed restrictions, Robinson adapted by migrating to alternative platforms, creating multiple accounts, and leveraging encrypted messaging apps. Yet each adaptation came with diminishing returns. The reach that had once been extraordinary became fragmented, and the constant fight against digital suppression consumed more energy than the platforms themselves could provide.

Despite these setbacks, the digital battlefield solidified Robinson's influence in a way the streets never could. Videos, memes, and viral posts extended his message far beyond local rallies or media appearances. For younger audiences, social media was the primary lens through which they encountered him, framing him as a relentless campaigner and digital insurgent. For critics, it was a new form of activism that defied traditional regulation, raising questions about online accountability, the limits of free speech, and the responsibilities of global tech companies.

By 2018, it was clear that the digital stage had reshaped Robinson's activism. He was no longer merely a man reacting to events in Britain; he had become a figure capable of influencing debates across Europe and the United States. The online environment amplified every success, every controversy, and every legal entanglement. Yet it also exposed him to relentless scrutiny, with every post dissected, every word analysed, and every strategy critiqued.

The rise and fall of Robinson's social media empire demonstrated both the power and the volatility of the digital age. Platforms that had allowed him to speak to millions simultaneously could just as quickly silence him. But through this chaos, he learned a critical lesson: influence was no longer determined by proximity to power or physical presence, but by the ability to command attention across networks, continents, and algorithms. In the digital battlefield, Tommy Robinson had not just survived; he had reinvented himself as a figure whose reach could rival governments, media conglomerates, and traditional political parties.

CHAPTER 11

The Journalist Incident

The summer of 2018 marked a turning point in Tommy Robinson's life, one that would elevate him from a controversial activist to a figure of international debate. In Leeds, outside a courthouse, Robinson recorded a video that would become the flashpoint for his arrest, conviction, and the polarised perceptions that followed. The case involved a trial of individuals accused of grooming and sexual exploitation, a sensitive proceeding in which reporting restrictions were strictly enforced to protect the anonymity of victims. Robinson's decision to film outside the courthouse and broadcast online was immediate and calculated, aimed at drawing attention to a story he claimed mainstream media were ignoring.

Robinson's video quickly went viral, amassing hundreds of thousands of views within hours. In it, he described the case in blunt terms, emphasising his belief that justice was being obstructed and that authorities were failing the victims. His supporters hailed the act as courageous, an exposure of wrongdoing and a challenge to institutional complacency. Critics and the courts viewed it differently: the video was seen as violating strict reporting restrictions designed to safeguard the integrity of the trial and the anonymity of victims. The law, they argued, could not tolerate such breaches, no matter the motivation.

The legal consequences were swift and severe. Robinson was arrested outside the courthouse and charged with contempt of court. The trial itself was fast-tracked, a reflection of both the seriousness of the offence and the public attention surrounding it. The courtroom became a media circus in miniature, with journalists and supporters packed in, eager to witness a case that had already sparked nationwide discussion. Robinson defended his actions vigorously, claiming he had a right to inform the public about crimes that the authorities had allegedly neglected to highlight. He framed the case as a matter of free speech, portraying himself as a citizen confronting institutional failure.

To supporters, this was the moment that transformed Robinson from activist to martyr. Campaigns for his release erupted online, with hashtags, petitions, and viral posts portraying the conviction as politically motivated persecution. The narrative was straightforward: here was a man who had dared to speak uncomfortable truths and who was being punished not for breaking the law in spirit, but for challenging the establishment. The imagery of a courtroom, police officers, and a defendant facing serious consequences fueled a sense of injustice that transcended Britain, resonating with audiences in Europe, the United States, and beyond.

International attention intensified the stakes. Right-wing commentators, activists, and media outlets framed Robinson's imprisonment as an attack on free speech itself. The case was cited in debates about press freedom, digital reporting, and the limits of citizen journalism. To many, Robinson had become emblematic of a global struggle: the tension between State authority, media control, and the individual's right to speak, even in contentious circumstances. Supporters across borders rallied in solidarity, drawing attention to his legal plight and amplifying his story far beyond the confines of a single British courtroom.

Yet the reality inside the courtroom and beyond was more complex. Judges and prosecutors emphasised the necessity of reporting restrictions to ensure the fair administration of justice. The sensitivity of cases involving sexual exploitation and minors demanded careful adherence to the law. Robinson's conviction was not merely punitive; it was framed as a protective measure, ensuring that victims and witnesses would not be further harmed by premature exposure. The legal system, in this reading, was acting according to principles rather than personal animus.

The incident crystallised a paradox that would define Robinson's public persona. To one audience, he was a hero, a defender of transparency and accountability. To another, he was a lawbreaker, flouting rules designed to uphold justice and protect the vulnerable. The courtroom event and the conviction that followed amplified the divide between supporters and critics, turning a single act of filming into a defining chapter of his life.

In the aftermath, Robinson's status as a "free speech martyr" was cemented. Campaigns for his release continued for months, with online petitions, social media campaigns, and international commentaries keeping the story alive. The incident highlighted the power of digital platforms to shape narratives and influence public perception, demonstrating that even imprisonment could serve as a stage for visibility and activism.

By the Time he left the courthouse, the Tommy Robinson story had entered a new phase. He was no longer merely a British activist or former EDL leader; he had become a global symbol of the tensions between law, free speech, and the public's right to information. The journalist incident would define his image for years to come, reinforcing his notoriety and solidifying his role as a lightning rod in debates over the boundaries of activism, legality, and moral authority.

CHAPTER 12

The Political Arena

Tommy Robinson's ambitions extended beyond activism and digital influence; he sought to enter the formal structures of political power. By the late 2010s, he had become a nationally recognised figure, a polarising voice whose notoriety guaranteed attention wherever he spoke. Naturally, the transition from street campaigns and social media prominence to electoral politics seemed a logical next step. Yet the path was fraught with challenges that revealed both the limitations of his persona and the rigidity of Britain's mainstream political system.

Robinson's first forays into formal politics were cautious, exploratory attempts rather than full-scale campaigns. He engaged with the United Kingdom Independence Party (UKIP), a populist, anti-immigration party that had enjoyed moments of prominence under

Nigel Farage. UKIP appeared, at first glance, to be a natural ally: Robinson shared its scepticism toward immigration policy, concern over Islamist extremism, and populist rhetoric. Yet the alignment was uneasy. Farage and party leaders were acutely aware of the risks of formal association. While Robinson brought visibility, he also carried a history of street violence, legal troubles, and polarising statements that could alienate mainstream voters.

Despite these tensions, Robinson flirted with candidacy. His name circulated in discussions about the European Parliament elections and local political contests. Supporters encouraged him to run, seeing electoral office as a path to legitimise his message and wield influence through official channels rather than protests. Campaign literature emphasised public safety, freedom of speech, and a tough stance on Islamist extremism. Yet the history that had made him a household name also made him unacceptable to established parties, and he faced repeated resistance when attempting to gain formal endorsements or nominations.

The reasons for rejection were multifaceted. Mainstream political parties, across the spectrum, feared reputational damage from being associated with them. Robinson's legal record, contentious rhetoric, and persistent conflicts with authorities rendered him politically toxic. Media scrutiny of any formal political engagement would be immediate and intense, magnifying past controversies. In effect, Robinson had built a brand of influence outside the political system that simultaneously elevated him and precluded acceptance within it.

Undeterred, Robinson explored alternative avenues. He attended events with populist and anti-establishment movements across Europe, forging informal connections with like-minded figures in Germany, France, and Italy. These networks recognised him as a peer: a man who had built a following independently of party machinery, who could mobilise support through grassroots activism and digital influence. Yet these international ties, while symbolically powerful, did little to secure a foothold in British electoral politics. National campaigns demanded organisation, funding, and legitimacy that Robinson could not fully command.

Robinson's attempts in the political arena also illuminated a broader truth about populist movements in Britain. While street-level activism, viral media presence, and digital campaigning can secure attention, they cannot automatically translate into electoral success. Political power required negotiation, coalition-building, and compromise—qualities that Robinson had historically avoided. His brand thrived on confrontation, principled defiance, and uncompromising rhetoric. Politics, by contrast, demanded pragmatism, message discipline, and the ability to absorb criticism without alienating the base. The mismatch was fundamental.

Yet even in failure, Robinson's political ambitions shaped public discourse. His presence forced mainstream parties to address issues he highlighted, particularly concerns over immigration, Islamist extremism, and community safety. Politicians debated policies in ways they might not have otherwise, aware that Robinson's activism could mobilise voters dissatisfied with traditional platforms. While he never secured elected office, his influence within the political sphere remained real: a cautionary, polarising force compelling others to respond.

By the end of this period, Robinson had learned a critical lesson: his power lay not in formal authority but in visibility, agitation, and the ability to dominate narratives outside traditional structures. The political arena rejected him, not because he lacked ideas, but because he embodied a form of influence that was uncontrollable, unpredictable, and uncomfortable for a system built on order and compromise. The streets, the courts, and the digital platforms had made him a public figure; politics, with its rules and constraints, offered him no refuge.

In this sense, Tommy Robinson's engagement with formal politics was both an experiment and a reaffirmation of his identity. He discovered the limits of institutional power, the barriers imposed by history and reputation, and the enduring appeal of outsider status. He remained a voice that could not be elected but could not be ignored—a man whose ambitions, if thwarted in office, were magnified in the court of public opinion.

CHAPTER 13

The Global Stage

By the late 2010s, Tommy Robinson had transcended the borders of Britain. What began as local activism in Luton and public spectacles on the streets had evolved into a presence on the international stage, drawing attention from politicians, media figures, and activist networks across Europe and the United States. Robinson's notoriety, amplified by legal battles and digital influence, gave him a profile that was no longer merely national—it was transnational.

Connections with like-minded populists abroad emerged organically. Figures in Europe, from Germany to France and Italy, recognised Robinson as a peer who had built a following independently of traditional party machinery. He was invited to speak at rallies, debates, and conferences, where his perspectives on Islam, immigration, and free speech resonated with audiences already primed to embrace anti-establishment narratives. These interactions were often symbolic, reinforcing his status as part of a broader network of populist voices challenging mainstream politics.

Across the Atlantic, Robinson became a figure of fascination within American right-wing circles. Interviews with conservative media, appearances at events, and commentary on transnational migration issues positioned him as a cautionary yet inspiring example of grassroots activism. In the United States, where free speech debates are particularly pronounced, Robinson was often framed as a defender of expression against what some commentators described as "media bias" or institutional suppression. His experiences in Britain became a lens through which American audiences interpreted questions of censorship, activism, and legal boundaries.

Yet international visibility came with complications. Some countries welcomed him with open arms, while others imposed restrictions, bans, or denials of entry. European authorities, particularly in nations sensitive to public order and extremist mobilisation, closely monitored his movements. Invitations could be rescinded at the last moment, conferences could refuse him a stage, and events occasionally became sites of protest and confrontation. Robinson's global ambitions highlighted the tension between symbolic recognition and practical limitations, illustrating the fine line between celebrity and ostracism on the world stage.

Robinson's presence abroad also underscored the symbolic dimension of his influence. He was no longer simply a man advocating in local or national debates; he had become an icon, a lightning rod around which controversies, loyalties, and narratives coalesced. International supporters framed him as a pioneer in a global struggle for free speech, a model for activists navigating media scrutiny, legal obstacles, and public hostility. Opponents, meanwhile, emphasised the dangers of importing polarising rhetoric across borders, warning that his ideas could inflame tensions far from Britain.

In this period, the digital and the physical intertwined seamlessly. Social media allowed Robinson to broadcast international appearances in real Time, amplifying their impact and extending their reach beyond those physically present. Viral videos, interviews, and online campaigns ensured that each event, whether in Europe or the United States, became part of an ongoing narrative of resistance, defiance, and controversy. For supporters, the global stage validated his significance; for critics, it magnified the threat they associated with his rhetoric.

Through these international interactions, Robinson's life became a case study in modern populist influence. He demonstrated how an individual could leverage digital tools, personal branding, and high-profile confrontations to exert authority without formal office or institutional power. His visibility on the world stage reflected both the opportunities and the constraints of modern activism: he could inspire, provoke, and mobilise, yet he remained subject to the limits imposed by law, logistics, and the perceptions of foreign governments.

By the end of this period, Tommy Robinson had firmly established himself as a figure of global significance. His narrative was no longer confined to Luton streets, British courtrooms, or the English Defence League. He had become a symbol—contentious, polarising, and impossible to ignore—whose presence in international debates forced nations, media organisations, and activists alike to confront the complexities of free speech, populism, and the enduring tensions between citizen activism and institutional authority.

CHAPTER 14

Family, Faith, and Identity

Behind the headlines, court cases, and viral videos existed a private man whose life was shaped by far more than activism and controversy. Tommy Robinson's public persona—a confrontational, unflinching figure challenging institutions, the media, and political establishments—often overshadowed the complexities of his personal life; yet, understanding these facets is essential to grasping the motivations, resilience, and contradictions that defined him.

Family life, in particular, offered both grounding and complication. As a father, Robinson faced the constant tension of balancing parental responsibility with the relentless demands of public life. His children's upbringing unfolded against a backdrop of media scrutiny, legal battles, and social polarisation. Everyday concerns—school, safety, and emotional stability—were amplified by his notoriety. For supporters, Robinson's role as a father humanised him, a reminder that even polarising figures live with ordinary responsibilities and vulnerabilities. For critics, the family context underscored the stark contrasts between personal morality and public behaviour, raising questions about influence, example, and the pressures placed on loved ones caught in the spotlight.

Robinson's relationships within his family reflected his broader struggles with identity and authority. His Irish heritage, working-class upbringing, and early life in Luton shaped a worldview rooted in loyalty, resilience, and suspicion of centralised power. These elements influenced how he interacted with children, partners, and extended family. Fatherhood was not a retreat from activism but a lens through which he viewed society: concerns for the safety and future of his family often intertwined with his broader critiques of governance, multicultural policy, and community cohesion. Parenting became both a moral compass and a source of tension, shaping decisions about public engagement, risk, and visibility.

Faith also played a complex role in Robinson's life. Raised in a context influenced by cultural Catholicism and family tradition, his spiritual identity evolved in tandem with his public persona. Religion offered both a grounding philosophy and a framework for understanding justice, morality, and personal responsibility. Publicly, Robinson often framed his arguments around concepts of right and wrong, accountability, and societal order; yet, these principles were also deeply entwined with his personal beliefs about ethics and faith. Observers noted that his moral framework—shaped by religious and cultural tenets—was inseparable from the rhetoric he employed in activism, from his critiques of institutional authority to his conception of civic duty.

Identity, however, was never static. Robinson's sense of self was continually negotiated across multiple spheres: as a son of a working-class family, as a father, as a public agitator, and as a man navigating legal, social, and digital battlegrounds. Each role came with its own expectations, constraints, and responsibilities. Balancing these identities required constant adaptation. At times, the public figure overshadowed the private man; at other times, the pressures of personal life informed public actions. His choices, strategies, and rhetoric cannot be fully understood without acknowledging the interplay between these spheres.

The tension between public and private identity was most acute during periods of legal peril. While supporters focused on his resilience and defiance, Robinson's family bore witness to the emotional, psychological, and practical toll of repeated arrests, imprisonment, and global scrutiny. Fatherhood, partnership, and personal belief became both sources of strength and reminders of vulnerability. Maintaining integrity, providing care, and fostering stability required navigating a landscape that few outside his immediate circle could imagine.

By examining Robinson through the lenses of family, faith, and identity, a more nuanced understanding emerges. He was not merely a figure of controversy or a digital provocateur; he was a man negotiating the weight of responsibility, belief, and personal history. These private dimensions offer insight into why he persisted despite public hostility, legal challenges, and social polarisation. They reveal the motivations behind his actions, the moral convictions that guided his choices, and the human consequences of living life under relentless scrutiny.

Ultimately, Tommy Robinson's story cannot be fully comprehended without recognising the man behind the headlines. His family, his faith, and his deeply ingrained sense of identity were the quiet engines driving a life lived at the intersection of defiance and responsibility, notoriety and intimacy, ideology and humanity. The public battles, media storms, and legal confrontations were only one dimension of a life profoundly shaped by personal belief, familial loyalty, and the enduring quest to define oneself in a complex and often hostile world.

CHAPTER 15

Supporters and Opponents

Tommy Robinson's life has always existed in stark contrast: admiration on one side, condemnation on the other. Understanding his impact requires examining the duality of public perception—the fervent loyalty he inspires among certain Britons and the organised opposition he faces from political, media, and activist circles.

To his supporters, Robinson embodies a voice they feel is missing in Britain's public discourse. Many working-class Britons, especially in towns like Luton, see him as someone who articulates frustrations that mainstream politicians and media often ignore. Issues of immigration, community safety, and cultural change resonate personally, and Robinson's rhetoric frames these concerns in a way that validates lived experiences.

For supporters, he is a defender of ordinary citizens, a man willing to confront institutions they perceive as indifferent or hostile. His directness, his willingness to challenge authority, and his resilience under legal and media pressure create an aura of authenticity and courage. Social media amplifies this resonance, allowing supporters to form virtual communities where Robinson's messages are repeated, debated, and celebrated.

Yet for every supporter, there exists an equally organised opposition. Critics view him as a figure whose rhetoric fuels division, fear, and, at times, hostility. Political leaders across the spectrum, from local councils to Parliament, have publicly denounced his methods and messaging. Media outlets dissect his statements, highlight legal violations, and frame his activism as dangerous or extreme. Activist groups, particularly those advocating for multicultural cohesion, civil rights, and anti-racism, mobilise campaigns to counter his influence. This opposition is not merely reactive; it is strategic, designed to limit his reach, challenge his narratives, and shape public perception.

The tension between supporters and opponents has created a self-reinforcing cycle. Legal actions, court cases, and media scrutiny often strengthen his base, who interpret these events as persecution, reinforcing loyalty and engagement. Conversely, each public statement, viral video, or controversial action intensifies the opposition, prompting broader media coverage, political debate, and organised campaigns to counter his influence. Robinson exists at the centre of a dynamic feedback loop, where every move magnifies both admiration and resistance.

The media plays a particularly decisive role in this duality. Headlines, editorials, and broadcasts frame him in ways that influence public perception far beyond the immediate audience of his speeches or posts. Some outlets emphasise the sensational aspects—protests, arrests, confrontations—while others scrutinise his rhetoric, legal history, and political ambitions. For supporters, media attacks often validate claims of bias and suppression; for opponents, coverage highlights the potential societal risks of his influence. In both cases, Robinson's image is amplified, shaped as much by representation as by action.

Political forces further shape the battlefield. Members of Parliament, party strategists, and policymakers weigh the potential impact of Robinson on electoral politics, social cohesion, and law enforcement priorities. Official condemnation, legislative attention, or public warnings become part of the broader narrative surrounding him. Even unsuccessful attempts at political engagement influence perceptions, framing him as either a legitimate voice marginalised by establishment politics or as a dangerous agitator whose ambitions must be contained.

Activists and community organisations provide the third axis of opposition. Grassroots campaigns, public demonstrations, and social media mobilisations target both his actions and the narratives he promotes. By documenting events, countering misinformation, and fostering public debate, these groups aim to limit his influence and protect communities he is accused of misrepresenting or antagonising. In doing so, they contribute to the highly polarised environment in which Robinson operates, where every statement or appearance becomes a point of contestation.

Ultimately, Tommy Robinson's story cannot be understood without acknowledging this duality. He exists simultaneously as a symbol of defiance and a figure of concern, a lightning rod around which loyalty and opposition coalesce. The interplay between supporters and opponents defines much of his public life, shaping strategy, messaging, and personal choices. It is a relationship that amplifies his influence, reinforces divisions in public opinion, and ensures that his life remains both intensely scrutinised and profoundly consequential.

Robinson's public battles are inseparable from the reactions they provoke. Supporters, opponents, media, politicians, and activists collectively construct the narrative that surrounds him, ensuring that his presence—whether celebrated or vilified—remains central to debates over identity, security, and public discourse in modern Britain.

CHAPTER 16

A Mirror of Britain

Tommy Robinson's life, with all its controversies, legal battles, and global attention, serves as more than a biography of a single individual. It is, in many ways, a lens through which the fractures and tensions of modern Britain are revealed. His rise, conflicts, and enduring notoriety reflect broader societal struggles over identity, governance, and the balance between freedom and order.

At the heart of this narrative is the debate over immigration and multiculturalism. Robinson's activism often centred on communities that felt marginalised, threatened, or ignored amidst rapid demographic changes. For many of his supporters, these concerns were personal, tied to local experiences of economic competition, crime, and cultural displacement. Robinson articulated these anxieties in ways that resonated with ordinary citizens who felt their voices were unheard. In doing so, he became both a conduit and a catalyst, channeling diffuse frustrations into collective awareness and mobilisation.

Yet his prominence also magnified the challenges of multiculturalism in Britain. Critics argue that his rhetoric exacerbated divisions, fostering a "us versus them" mentality that eroded social cohesion. Communities became polarised, conversations became contentious, and debates over policy were infused with emotion, suspicion, and fear. Robinson's activism, whether intentionally or not, illuminated the delicate balance between acknowledging legitimate concerns and stoking collective anxiety—a balance that Britain, like many democracies, continues to struggle with.

National identity emerges as another critical theme. Robinson's story underscores the tension between traditional conceptions of Britishness and the evolving realities of a pluralistic society. Questions of language, culture, religion, and belonging are never abstract in his narrative; they are concrete forces shaping neighbourhoods, institutions, and political discourse. His supporters often frame their arguments around preserving a shared heritage, while opponents emphasise inclusivity, human rights, and equality. The resulting debate is both intensely local and profoundly national, reflecting a society grappling with its own sense of self in the twenty-first century.

Robinson's life also exemplifies the costs of populist anger in a democracy. Populist figures thrive on emotion, grievance, and the perception of neglect by traditional institutions. They can mobilise audiences, disrupt conventional politics, and draw attention to overlooked issues. Yet they also introduce volatility. Robinson's campaigns, social media influence, and public clashes with authorities demonstrate how populist energy can amplify polarisation, strain legal and social frameworks, and create enduring public conflict. Supporters often see courage and advocacy; critics, on the other hand, see destabilisation and extremism. In this duality, Robinson's life reflects the broader challenge of harnessing citizen energy without allowing it to fracture civic cohesion.

Legal entanglements, media battles, and international attention further highlight Britain's struggles with transparency, accountability, and freedom of expression. Robinson's arrests and court cases, while personal experiences, also became public tests of institutional integrity. They prompted debates about proportionality, censorship, and the limits of activism, illustrating the tension between individual liberty and societal responsibility. Britain's response to him, in law and culture, reveals the competing pressures faced by a democratic society trying to balance rights, security, and social harmony.

In many ways, Robinson's story is less about one man and more about the mirror he holds up to Britain. Through him, the nation confronts its anxieties, divides, and unresolved questions about identity, governance, and community. His life illustrates how local grievances can escalate into national debates, how digital platforms magnify controversy, and how populist figures can simultaneously inspire loyalty and provoke fear.

Epilogue

The Polarising Legacy

Tommy Robinson's life is a story of contradictions, conflicts, and relentless visibility. He is simultaneously admired and reviled, celebrated as a defender of free speech and condemned as a provocateur whose rhetoric fuels division. The trajectory of his life—from the streets of Luton to the global stage—offers more than a biography of an individual; it is a prism through which the complexities of modern Britain are refracted, revealing the tensions, anxieties, and debates that define the nation today.

Robinson's legacy cannot be measured simply by legal records, social media followers, or international headlines. It is shaped by the emotional and ideological currents he mobilised. Supporters see him as a principled truth-teller, a man willing to challenge powerful institutions, expose uncomfortable realities, and give voice to communities they feel are overlooked or silenced. They view his arrests, court battles, and digital controversies as evidence of persecution, proof that the establishment fears his influence. For them, Robinson embodies courage, resilience, and the refusal to compromise principles for comfort or approval.

To critics, however, Robinson represents the dangers of populist anger unrestrained by accountability. His confrontational methods, often accompanied by incendiary rhetoric and repeated legal entanglements, are perceived as destabilising forces within society. He is seen as a symbol of polarisation, a figure whose activism exacerbates division, fosters fear, and undermines the cohesion of democratic institutions. Media outlets, political leaders, and activist organisations have sought to contextualise his influence within broader debates about extremism, social harmony, and the limits of free expression.

The duality of Robinson's perception underscores a broader societal truth: Britain itself is a nation in flux. Debates over immigration, multiculturalism, national identity, and community cohesion are ongoing and unresolved. Robinson's prominence highlights both the grievances of ordinary citizens and the challenges governments, media, and institutions face in addressing them constructively. He is, in essence, a mirror of Britain—a reflection of the nation's anxieties, divisions, and unresolved questions about who it is and who it wants to be.

At the same Time, Robinson's life illuminates the transformative power of the digital age. Social media, viral videos, and online networks enabled him to bypass traditional gatekeepers, reaching audiences nationwide and globally. He demonstrated that influence need not rely on formal political office or institutional legitimacy. Yet the same platforms that amplified his voice also subjected him to unprecedented scrutiny, bans, and algorithmic suppression. The digital battlefield that made him a global figure also created vulnerabilities, illustrating the precarious nature of influence in the twenty-first century.

Robinson's global visibility also raises questions about the intersection of national issues and international discourse. His experiences with right-wing activists in Europe and the United States show how domestic controversies can become transnational symbols, feeding debates about freedom of speech, populist movements, and cultural identity far beyond Britain's borders. He became a cautionary tale and a rallying figure, depending on the perspective, demonstrating how the actions of one individual can resonate far beyond local or national contexts.

Yet beyond the public persona—the activist, the provocateur, the digital insurgent—exists the private man. Fatherhood, faith, and personal identity shaped his choices, his resilience, and his worldview. These dimensions offer insight into why he persisted in the face of legal, social, and political challenges. They remind us that behind every headline and viral video lies a human being negotiating fear, responsibility, and the consequences of living under unrelenting scrutiny.

The lasting question surrounding Tommy Robinson is not simply whether his actions were right or wrong, but what his life reveals about the society that produced him. How does a nation balance freedom and order, debate and civility, anger and empathy? How does democracy accommodate voices that challenge institutions without undermining cohesion? Robinson's story does not provide definitive answers, but it forces Britain—and observers worldwide—to confront these questions with clarity, urgency, and discomfort.

Tommy Robinson's legacy is inseparable from the fractures and debates of contemporary Britain. He will remain a polarising figure, a symbol of defiance, and a subject of intense scrutiny. But he is also a reminder that public life, activism, and identity are deeply intertwined, and that the future of a nation is inseparable from the voices that demand to be heard. His life reflects the costs and consequences of populist anger, the power of digital influence, and the enduring challenge of reconciling freedom with responsibility in a complex, modern democracy.

Whether admired or condemned, Robinson has left an indelible mark on Britain. His story, controversial and contested, endures as both a warning and a mirror—a reflection of a nation grappling with change, conflict, and the enduring question of who it truly is.

Printed in Dunstable, United Kingdom